This Travel Journal Belongs To:

_____

_____

_____

☀ Today we went to: _____

❄ Date: _____   Location: _____

Today Is: Monday Tuesday Wednesday
Thursday Friday Saturday Sunday

👓 Weather 👓

Temperature: _____

_____
_____
_____

★ Draw the best thing about today ★

List something that you

heard: _____

smelled: _____

ate: _____

☂ What did you see or do? _____

_____
_____
_____
_____
_____
_____
_____
_____
_____

Today's Overall Rating

☆ ☆ ☆ ☆ ☆

☀ **Today we went to:** _____

❄ **Date:** _____   **Location:** _____

Today Is: Monday Tuesday Wednesday
Thursday Friday Saturday Sunday

👓**Weather**👓

Temperature: _____

_____
_____
_____

⭐ **Draw the best thing about today** ⭐

List something that you

heard: _____

smelled: _____

ate: _____

☂ **What did you see or do?** _____

_____

_____

_____

_____

_____

_____

_____

_____

Today's Overall Rating
☆ ☆ ☆ ☆ ☆

☀ Today we went to: _____

❄ Date: _____   Location: _____

Today Is: Monday Tuesday Wednesday
Thursday Friday Saturday Sunday

🕶 Weather 🕶

Temperature: _____

☀ ⛅ ☁ 🌧

_____
_____
_____

★ Draw the best thing about today ★

List something that you

heard: _____

smelled: _____

ate: _____

☂ What did you see or do? _____

_____

_____

_____

_____

_____

_____

_____

_____

_____

_____

Today's Overall Rating

☆ ☆ ☆ ☆ ☆

☀ Today we went to: _____

❄ Date: _____   Location: _____

Today Is: Monday Tuesday Wednesday
Thursday Friday Saturday Sunday

🕶 Weather 🕶

Temperature: _____

_____
_____
_____

★ Draw the best thing about today ★

List something that you

heard: _____

smelled: _____

ate: _____

☂ What did you see or do? _____

_____
_____
_____
_____
_____
_____
_____
_____
_____

Today's Overall Rating
☆ ☆ ☆ ☆ ☆

☀ **Today we went to:** _____

❄ **Date:** _____ **Location:** _____

Today Is: Monday Tuesday Wednesday
Thursday Friday Saturday Sunday

Weather

Temperature: _____

_____
_____
_____

★ **Draw the best thing about today** ★

List something that you

heard: _____

smelled: _____

ate: _____

☂ **What did you see or do?** _____

_____
_____
_____
_____
_____
_____
_____
_____

Today's Overall Rating
☆ ☆ ☆ ☆ ☆

☀ Today we went to: _____

❄ Date: _____   Location: _____

Today Is: Monday Tuesday Wednesday
Thursday Friday Saturday Sunday

🕶 Weather 🕶

Temperature: _____

_____
_____
_____

★ Draw the best thing about today ★

List something that you

heard: _____

smelled: _____

ate: _____

☂ What did you see or do?_____

_____
_____
_____
_____
_____
_____
_____
_____
_____
_____

Today's Overall Rating
☆ ☆ ☆ ☆ ☆

☀ Today we went to: _____

❄ Date: _____   Location: _____

Today Is: Monday Tuesday Wednesday
Thursday Friday Saturday Sunday

🕶 Weather 🕶

Temperature: _____

_____
_____
_____

★ Draw the best thing about today ★

List something that you

heard: _____

smelled: _____

ate: _____

☂ What did you see or do? _____

_____
_____
_____
_____
_____
_____
_____
_____
_____

Today's Overall Rating

☆ ☆ ☆ ☆ ☆

☀ Today we went to: _____

❄ Date: _____ Location: _____

Today Is: Monday Tuesday Wednesday
Thursday Friday Saturday Sunday

🕶 **Weather** 🕶

Temperature: _____

_____
_____
_____

⭐ Draw the best thing about today ⭐

List something that you

heard: _____

smelled: _____

ate: _____

☂ What did you see or do?_____

_____
_____
_____
_____
_____
_____
_____
_____
_____

Today's Overall Rating
☆ ☆ ☆ ☆ ☆

☀ Today we went to: _____

❄ Date: _____ Location: _____

Today Is: Monday Tuesday Wednesday
Thursday Friday Saturday Sunday

🕶Weather🕶

Temperature: _____

_____
_____
_____

★ Draw the best thing about today ★

List something that you

heard: _____

smelled: _____

ate: _____

☂ What did you see or do?_____

_____
_____
_____
_____
_____
_____
_____
_____
_____

Today's Overall Rating
☆ ☆ ☆ ☆ ☆

☀ Today we went to: _____

❄ Date: _____   Location: _____

Today Is: Monday Tuesday Wednesday
Thursday Friday Saturday Sunday

Weather

Temperature: _____

_____
_____
_____

★ Draw the best thing about today ★

List something that you

heard: _____

smelled: _____

ate: _____

☂ What did you see or do?_____

_____
_____
_____
_____
_____
_____
_____
_____
_____

Today's Overall Rating

☆ ☆ ☆ ☆ ☆

☀ Today we went to: _____

❄ Date: _____   Location: _____

Today Is: Monday Tuesday Wednesday
Thursday Friday Saturday Sunday

🕶 Weather 🕶

Temperature: _____

_____
_____
_____

★ Draw the best thing about today ★

List something that you

heard: _____

smelled: _____

ate: _____

☂ What did you see or do?_____

_____
_____
_____
_____
_____
_____
_____
_____
_____

Today's Overall Rating

☆ ☆ ☆ ☆ ☆

☀ **Today we went to:** _____

❄ **Date:** _____   **Location:** _____

**Today Is: Monday Tuesday Wednesday
Thursday Friday Saturday Sunday**

🕶**Weather**🕶

Temperature: _____

_____
_____
_____

⭐ **Draw the best thing about today** ⭐

List something that you

heard: _____

smelled: _____

ate: _____

☂ **What did you see or do?**_____

_____
_____
_____
_____
_____
_____
_____
_____
_____
_____

Today's Overall Rating
☆ ☆ ☆ ☆ ☆

☀ **Today we went to:** _____

❄ **Date:** _____ **Location:** _____

Today Is: Monday Tuesday Wednesday Thursday Friday Saturday Sunday

👓 **Weather** 👓

Temperature: _____

☀ 🌤 ☁ 🌧

_____
_____
_____

★ Draw the best thing about today ★

List something that you

heard: _____

smelled: _____

ate: _____

☂ **What did you see or do?** _____

_____
_____
_____
_____
_____
_____
_____
_____
_____

Today's Overall Rating

☆ ☆ ☆ ☆ ☆

☀ Today we went to: _____

❄ Date: _____   Location: _____

Today Is: Monday Tuesday Wednesday
Thursday Friday Saturday Sunday

🕶Weather🕶

Temperature: _____

_____
_____
_____

★ Draw the best thing about today ★

List something that you

heard: _____

smelled: _____

ate: _____

☂ What did you see or do?_____

_____
_____
_____
_____
_____
_____
_____
_____

Today's Overall Rating
☆ ☆ ☆ ☆ ☆

☀ **Today we went to:** _____

❄ **Date:** _____ **Location:** _____

Today Is: Monday Tuesday Wednesday
Thursday Friday Saturday Sunday

🕶 **Weather** 🕶

Temperature: _____

_____
_____
_____

⭐ **Draw the best thing about today** ⭐

List something that you

heard: _____

smelled: _____

ate: _____

☂ **What did you see or do?** _____

_____
_____
_____
_____
_____
_____
_____
_____

Today's Overall Rating
☆ ☆ ☆ ☆ ☆

☀ **Today we went to:** _____

❄ **Date:** _____ **Location:** _____

Today Is: Monday Tuesday Wednesday Thursday Friday Saturday Sunday

👓**Weather**👓

Temperature: _____

_____
_____
_____

★ Draw the best thing about today ★

List something that you

heard: _____

smelled: _____

ate: _____

☂ **What did you see or do?** _____

_____
_____
_____
_____
_____
_____
_____
_____
_____

Today's Overall Rating
☆ ☆ ☆ ☆ ☆

☀ Today we went to: _____

❄ Date: _____ Location: _____

Today Is: Monday Tuesday Wednesday
Thursday Friday Saturday Sunday

🕶 Weather 🕶

Temperature: _____

_____
_____
_____

★ Draw the best thing about today ★

List something that you

heard: _____

smelled: _____

ate: _____

☂ What did you see or do? _____

_____
_____
_____
_____
_____
_____
_____
_____
_____

Today's Overall Rating
☆ ☆ ☆ ☆ ☆

☀ **Today we went to:** _____

❄ **Date:** _____   **Location:** _____

Today Is: Monday Tuesday Wednesday
Thursday Friday Saturday Sunday

🕶 **Weather** 🕶

Temperature: _____

_____
_____
_____

★ **Draw the best thing about today** ★

List something that you

heard: _____

smelled: _____

ate: _____

☂ **What did you see or do?** _____

_____
_____
_____
_____
_____
_____
_____
_____
_____
_____

Today's Overall Rating
☆ ☆ ☆ ☆ ☆

☀ Today we went to: _____

❄ Date: _____   Location: _____

Today Is: Monday Tuesday Wednesday
Thursday Friday Saturday Sunday

🕶 Weather 🕶

Temperature: _____

_____
_____
_____

⭐ Draw the best thing about today ⭐

List something that you

heard: _____

smelled: _____

ate: _____

☂ What did you see or do? _____

_____

_____

_____

_____

_____

_____

_____

_____

_____

Today's Overall Rating

☆ ☆ ☆ ☆ ☆

☀ Today we went to: _____

❄ Date: _____   Location: _____

Today Is: Monday Tuesday Wednesday
Thursday Friday Saturday Sunday

👓 Weather 👓

Temperature: _____

☀ ⛅ ☁ 🌧

_____
_____
_____

⭐ Draw the best thing about today ⭐

List something that you

heard: _____

smelled: _____

ate: _____

☂ **What did you see or do?** _____

_____

_____

_____

_____

_____

_____

_____

_____

_____

Today's Overall Rating

☆ ☆ ☆ ☆ ☆

☀ Today we went to: _____

❄ Date: _____ Location: _____

Today Is: Monday Tuesday Wednesday
Thursday Friday Saturday Sunday

🕶 Weather 🕶

Temperature: _____

_____
_____
_____

★ Draw the best thing about today ★

List something that you

heard: _____

smelled: _____

ate: _____

☂ What did you see or do?_____

_____
_____
_____
_____
_____
_____
_____
_____
_____

Today's Overall Rating

☆ ☆ ☆ ☆ ☆

☀ Today we went to: _____

❄ Date: _____   Location: _____

Today Is: Monday Tuesday Wednesday
Thursday Friday Saturday Sunday

🕶 Weather 🕶

Temperature: _____

_____
_____
_____

★ Draw the best thing about today ★

List something that you

heard: _____

smelled: _____

ate: _____

☂ What did you see or do? _____

_____
_____
_____
_____
_____
_____
_____
_____
_____

Today's Overall Rating

☆ ☆ ☆ ☆ ☆

☀ Today we went to: _____

❄ Date: _____   Location: _____

Today Is: Monday Tuesday Wednesday
Thursday Friday Saturday Sunday

🕶 Weather 🕶

Temperature: _____

_____

_____

_____

★ Draw the best thing about today ★

List something that you

heard: _____

smelled: _____

ate: _____

☂ What did you see or do? _____

_____

_____

_____

_____

_____

_____

_____

_____

_____

Today's Overall Rating
☆ ☆ ☆ ☆ ☆

☀ Today we went to: _____

❄ Date: _____   Location: _____

Today Is: Monday Tuesday Wednesday
Thursday Friday Saturday Sunday

🕶Weather🕶

Temperature: _____

_____
_____
_____

★ Draw the best thing about today ★

List something that you

heard: _____

smelled: _____

ate: _____

☂ What did you see or do?_____

_____
_____
_____
_____
_____
_____
_____
_____
_____

Today's Overall Rating
☆ ☆ ☆ ☆ ☆

☀ Today we went to: _____

❄ Date: _____   Location: _____

Today Is: Monday Tuesday Wednesday
Thursday Friday Saturday Sunday

🕶 Weather 🕶

Temperature: _____

_____
_____
_____

★ Draw the best thing about today ★

List something that you

heard: _____

smelled: _____

ate: _____

☂ What did you see or do? _____

_____
_____
_____
_____
_____
_____
_____
_____
_____

Today's Overall Rating
☆ ☆ ☆ ☆ ☆

☀ Today we went to: _____

❄ Date: _____   Location: _____

Today Is: Monday Tuesday Wednesday
Thursday Friday Saturday Sunday

👓 Weather 👓

Temperature: _____

_____
_____
_____

★ Draw the best thing about today ★

List something that you

heard: _____

smelled: _____

ate: _____

☂ What did you see or do? _____

_____
_____
_____
_____
_____
_____
_____
_____
_____

Today's Overall Rating

☆ ☆ ☆ ☆ ☆

☀ Today we went to: _____

❄ Date: _____ Location: _____

Today Is: Monday Tuesday Wednesday
Thursday Friday Saturday Sunday

🕶 Weather 🕶

Temperature: _____

_____
_____
_____

★ Draw the best thing about today ★

List something that you

heard: _____

smelled: _____

ate: _____

☂ What did you see or do? _____

_____
_____
_____
_____
_____
_____
_____
_____
_____

Today's Overall Rating
☆ ☆ ☆ ☆ ☆

☀ **Today we went to:** _____

❄ **Date:** _____ **Location:** _____

Today Is: Monday Tuesday Wednesday Thursday Friday Saturday Sunday

👓 Weather 👓

Temperature: _____

_____
_____
_____

★ **Draw the best thing about today** ★

List something that you

heard: _____

smelled: _____

ate: _____

☂ **What did you see or do?** _____

_____

_____

_____

_____

_____

_____

_____

_____

_____

Today's Overall Rating

☆ ☆ ☆ ☆ ☆

☀ Today we went to: _____

❄ Date: _____ Location: _____

Today Is: Monday Tuesday Wednesday
Thursday Friday Saturday Sunday

👓 Weather 👓

Temperature: _____

_____
_____
_____

★ Draw the best thing about today ★

List something that you

heard: _____

smelled: _____

ate: _____

☂ What did you see or do? _____

_____
_____
_____
_____
_____
_____
_____
_____
_____

Today's Overall Rating
☆ ☆ ☆ ☆ ☆

☀ Today we went to: _____

❄ Date: _____   Location: _____

Today Is: Monday Tuesday Wednesday
Thursday Friday Saturday Sunday

🕶 Weather 🕶

Temperature: _____

_____
_____
_____

★ Draw the best thing about today ★

List something that you

heard: _____

smelled: _____

ate: _____

☂ What did you see or do?_____

_____
_____
_____
_____
_____
_____
_____
_____

Today's Overall Rating
☆ ☆ ☆ ☆ ☆

☀ Today we went to: _____

❄ Date: _____ Location: _____

Today Is: Monday Tuesday Wednesday
Thursday Friday Saturday Sunday

🕶 Weather 🕶

Temperature: _____

_____
_____
_____

★ Draw the best thing about today ★

List something that you

heard: _____

smelled: _____

ate: _____

☂ What did you see or do? _____

_____
_____
_____
_____
_____
_____
_____
_____
_____

Today's Overall Rating

☆ ☆ ☆ ☆ ☆

☀ Today we went to: _____

❄ Date: _____   Location: _____

Today Is: Monday Tuesday Wednesday
Thursday Friday Saturday Sunday

🕶 Weather 🕶

Temperature: _____

_____
_____
_____

★ Draw the best thing about today ★

List something that you

heard: _____

smelled: _____

ate: _____

☂ What did you see or do? _____

_____
_____
_____
_____
_____
_____
_____
_____

Today's Overall Rating
☆ ☆ ☆ ☆ ☆

☀ Today we went to: _____

❄ Date: _____ Location: _____

Today Is: Monday Tuesday Wednesday
Thursday Friday Saturday Sunday

🕶 Weather 🕶

Temperature: _____

_____
_____
_____

★ Draw the best thing about today ★

List something that you

heard: _____

smelled: _____

ate: _____

☂ What did you see or do? _____

_____
_____
_____
_____
_____
_____
_____
_____
_____

Today's Overall Rating
☆ ☆ ☆ ☆ ☆

☀ Today we went to: _____

❄ Date: _____   Location: _____

Today Is: Monday Tuesday Wednesday
Thursday Friday Saturday Sunday

🕶 Weather 🕶

Temperature: _____

_____
_____
_____

★ Draw the best thing about today ★

List something that you

heard: _____

smelled: _____

ate: _____

☂ What did you see or do? _____

_____

_____

_____

_____

_____

_____

_____

_____

Today's Overall Rating
☆ ☆ ☆ ☆ ☆

☀ Today we went to: _____

❆ Date: _____   Location: _____

Today Is: Monday Tuesday Wednesday
Thursday Friday Saturday Sunday

🕶 Weather 🕶

Temperature: _____

☀ ⛅ ☁ 🌧

_____
_____
_____

★ Draw the best thing about today ★

List something that you

heard: _____

smelled: _____

ate: _____

☔ What did you see or do? _____

_____
_____
_____
_____
_____
_____
_____
_____
_____

Today's Overall Rating

☆ ☆ ☆ ☆ ☆

☀ Today we went to: _____

❄ Date: _____   Location: _____

Today Is: Monday Tuesday Wednesday
Thursday Friday Saturday Sunday

🕶 Weather 🕶

Temperature: _____

_____
_____
_____

★ Draw the best thing about today ★

List something that you

heard: _____

smelled: _____

ate: _____

☂ What did you see or do? _____

_____
_____
_____
_____
_____
_____
_____
_____
_____
_____

Today's Overall Rating
☆ ☆ ☆ ☆ ☆

☀ Today we went to: _____

❄ Date: _____   Location: _____

Today Is: Monday Tuesday Wednesday
Thursday Friday Saturday Sunday

🕶Weather🕶

Temperature: _____

_____
_____
_____

★ Draw the best thing about today ★

List something that you

heard: _____

smelled: _____

ate: _____

☂ What did you see or do?_____

_____
_____
_____
_____
_____
_____
_____
_____

Today's Overall Rating
☆ ☆ ☆ ☆ ☆

☀ Today we went to: _____

❄ Date: _____ Location: _____

Today Is: Monday Tuesday Wednesday
Thursday Friday Saturday Sunday

🕶 Weather 🕶

Temperature: _____

_____
_____
_____

⭐ Draw the best thing about today ⭐

List something that you

heard: _____

smelled: _____

ate: _____

☂ What did you see or do?_____

_____
_____
_____
_____
_____
_____
_____
_____
_____

Today's Overall Rating
☆ ☆ ☆ ☆ ☆

☀ **Today we went to:** _____

❄ **Date:** _____ **Location:** _____

**Today Is: Monday Tuesday Wednesday
Thursday Friday Saturday Sunday**

🕶 **Weather** 🕶

Temperature: _____

_____
_____
_____

⭐ **Draw the best thing about today** ⭐

List something that you

heard: _____

smelled: _____

ate: _____

☂ **What did you see or do?** _____

_____
_____
_____
_____
_____
_____
_____
_____
_____

Today's Overall Rating

☆ ☆ ☆ ☆ ☆

☀ Today we went to: _____

❄ Date: _____ Location: _____

Today Is: Monday Tuesday Wednesday
Thursday Friday Saturday Sunday

👓 Weather 👓

Temperature: _____

_____
_____
_____

★ Draw the best thing about today ★

List something that you

heard: _____

smelled: _____

ate: _____

☂ What did you see or do? _____

_____
_____
_____
_____
_____
_____
_____
_____

Today's Overall Rating
☆ ☆ ☆ ☆ ☆

Today we went to: _____

Date: _____ Location: _____

Today Is: Monday Tuesday Wednesday
Thursday Friday Saturday Sunday

Weather

Temperature: _____

_____
_____
_____

★ Draw the best thing about today ★

List something that you

heard: _____

smelled: _____

ate: _____

What did you see or do? _____

_____
_____
_____
_____
_____
_____
_____
_____

Today's Overall Rating
☆ ☆ ☆ ☆ ☆

☀ Today we went to: _____

❄ Date: _____   Location: _____

Today Is: Monday Tuesday Wednesday
Thursday Friday Saturday Sunday

🕶 Weather 🕶

Temperature: _____

_____
_____
_____

★ Draw the best thing about today ★

List something that you

heard: _____

smelled: _____

ate: _____

☂ What did you see or do? _____

_____
_____
_____
_____
_____
_____
_____
_____
_____

Today's Overall Rating

☆ ☆ ☆ ☆ ☆

☀ **Today we went to:** _____

❄ **Date:** _____ **Location:** _____

Today Is: Monday Tuesday Wednesday
Thursday Friday Saturday Sunday

👓 **Weather** 👓

Temperature: _____

_____
_____
_____

★ **Draw the best thing about today** ★

List something that you

heard: _____

smelled: _____

ate: _____

☂ **What did you see or do?** _____

_____
_____
_____
_____
_____
_____
_____
_____

Today's Overall Rating
☆ ☆ ☆ ☆ ☆

☀ Today we went to: _____

❄ Date: _____ Location: _____

**Today Is: Monday Tuesday Wednesday
Thursday Friday Saturday Sunday**

👓 **Weather** 👓

Temperature: _____

_____

_____

_____

★ **Draw the best thing about today** ★

List something that you

heard: _____

smelled: _____

ate: _____

☂ **What did you see or do?**_____

_____

_____

_____

_____

_____

_____

_____

_____

_____

Today's Overall Rating

☆ ☆ ☆ ☆ ☆

☀ Today we went to: _____

❄ Date: _____   Location: _____

Today Is: Monday Tuesday Wednesday
Thursday Friday Saturday Sunday

👓 Weather 👓

Temperature: _____

_____
_____
_____

★ Draw the best thing about today ★

List something that you

heard: _____

smelled: _____

ate: _____

☂ What did you see or do? _____

_____
_____
_____
_____
_____
_____
_____
_____

Today's Overall Rating
☆ ☆ ☆ ☆ ☆

☀ Today we went to: _____

❄ Date: _____   Location: _____

Today Is: Monday Tuesday Wednesday
Thursday Friday Saturday Sunday

🕶 Weather 🕶

Temperature: _____

_____
_____
_____

★ Draw the best thing about today ★

List something that you

heard: _____

smelled: _____

ate: _____

☂ What did you see or do? _____

_____
_____
_____
_____
_____
_____
_____
_____
_____

Today's Overall Rating

☆ ☆ ☆ ☆ ☆

☀ Today we went to: _____

❄ Date: _____ Location: _____

Today Is: Monday Tuesday Wednesday
Thursday Friday Saturday Sunday

🕶 Weather 🕶

Temperature: _____

_____
_____
_____

★ Draw the best thing about today ★

List something that you

heard: _____

smelled: _____

ate: _____

☂ What did you see or do? _____

_____
_____
_____
_____
_____
_____
_____
_____
_____

Today's Overall Rating
☆ ☆ ☆ ☆ ☆

☀ Today we went to: _____

❄ Date: _____   Location: _____

Today Is: Monday Tuesday Wednesday
Thursday Friday Saturday Sunday

🕶 Weather 🕶

Temperature: _____

_____
_____
_____

★ Draw the best thing about today ★

List something that you

heard: _____

smelled: _____

ate: _____

☂ What did you see or do? _____

_____
_____
_____
_____
_____
_____
_____
_____
_____

Today's Overall Rating
☆ ☆ ☆ ☆ ☆

☀ Today we went to: _____

❄ Date: _____   Location: _____

Today Is: Monday Tuesday Wednesday
Thursday Friday Saturday Sunday

🕶 Weather 🕶

Temperature: _____

_____
_____
_____

★ Draw the best thing about today ★

List something that you

heard: _____

smelled: _____

ate: _____

☂ What did you see or do? _____

_____
_____
_____
_____
_____
_____
_____
_____
_____

Today's Overall Rating
☆ ☆ ☆ ☆ ☆

☀ Today we went to: _____

❄ Date: _____ Location: _____

Today Is: Monday Tuesday Wednesday
Thursday Friday Saturday Sunday

🕶 Weather 🕶

Temperature: _____

_____
_____
_____

★ Draw the best thing about today ★

List something that you

heard: _____

smelled: _____

ate: _____

☂ What did you see or do? _____

_____
_____
_____
_____
_____
_____
_____
_____
_____

Today's Overall Rating
☆ ☆ ☆ ☆ ☆

☀ Today we went to: _____

❄ Date: _____   Location: _____

Today Is: Monday Tuesday Wednesday
Thursday Friday Saturday Sunday

🕶 Weather 🕶

Temperature: _____

☀ ⛅ ☁ 🌧

_____

_____

_____

★ Draw the best thing about today ★

List something that you

heard: _____

smelled: _____

ate: _____

☂ What did you see or do? _____

_____

_____

_____

_____

_____

_____

_____

_____

_____

Today's Overall Rating

☆ ☆ ☆ ☆ ☆

Today we went to: _____

Date: _____ Location: _____

Today Is: Monday Tuesday Wednesday
Thursday Friday Saturday Sunday

Weather

Temperature: _____

_____
_____
_____

★ Draw the best thing about today ★

List something that you

heard: _____

smelled: _____

ate: _____

What did you see or do?_____

_____
_____
_____
_____
_____
_____
_____
_____
_____
_____

Today's Overall Rating

☆ ☆ ☆ ☆ ☆

☀ Today we went to: _____

❄ Date: _____ Location: _____

Today Is: Monday Tuesday Wednesday
Thursday Friday Saturday Sunday

🕶 Weather 🕶

Temperature: _____

_____
_____
_____

★ Draw the best thing about today ★

List something that you

heard: _____

smelled: _____

ate: _____

☂ What did you see or do? _____

_____
_____
_____
_____
_____
_____
_____
_____
_____

Today's Overall Rating
☆ ☆ ☆ ☆ ☆

☀ Today we went to: _____

❄ Date: _____ Location: _____

Today Is: Monday Tuesday Wednesday
Thursday Friday Saturday Sunday

👓 Weather 👓

Temperature: _____

_____
_____
_____

★ Draw the best thing about today ★

List something that you

heard: _____

smelled: _____

ate: _____

☂ What did you see or do? _____

_____
_____
_____
_____
_____
_____
_____
_____
_____

Today's Overall Rating
☆ ☆ ☆ ☆ ☆

☀ Today we went to: _____

❄ Date: _____ Location: _____

Today Is: Monday Tuesday Wednesday
Thursday Friday Saturday Sunday

👓 Weather 👓

Temperature: _____

_____
_____
_____

★ Draw the best thing about today ★

List something that you

heard: _____

smelled: _____

ate: _____

☂ What did you see or do? _____

_____
_____
_____
_____
_____
_____
_____
_____
_____

Today's Overall Rating

☆ ☆ ☆ ☆ ☆

☀ Today we went to: _____

❄ Date: _____ Location: _____

Today Is: Monday Tuesday Wednesday
Thursday Friday Saturday Sunday

🕶 Weather 🕶

Temperature: _____

_____
_____
_____

★ Draw the best thing about today ★

List something that you

heard: _____

smelled: _____

ate: _____

☂ What did you see or do? _____

_____
_____
_____
_____
_____
_____
_____
_____

_____

Today's Overall Rating
☆ ☆ ☆ ☆ ☆

☀ Today we went to: _____

❄ Date: _____ Location: _____

Today Is: Monday Tuesday Wednesday
Thursday Friday Saturday Sunday

🕶 Weather 🕶

Temperature: _____

_____
_____
_____

★ Draw the best thing about today ★

List something that you

heard: _____

smelled: _____

ate: _____

☂ What did you see or do? _____

_____

_____

_____

_____

_____

_____

_____

_____

_____

Today's Overall Rating
☆ ☆ ☆ ☆ ☆

☀ Today we went to: _____

❄ Date: _____   Location: _____

Today Is: Monday Tuesday Wednesday
Thursday Friday Saturday Sunday

🕶 Weather 🕶

Temperature: _____

_____
_____
_____

★ Draw the best thing about today ★

List something that you

heard: _____

smelled: _____

ate: _____

☂ What did you see or do? _____

_____
_____
_____
_____
_____
_____
_____
_____

Today's Overall Rating
☆ ☆ ☆ ☆ ☆

☀ Today we went to: _____

❄ Date: _____ Location: _____

Today Is: Monday Tuesday Wednesday
Thursday Friday Saturday Sunday

🕶Weather🕶

Temperature: _____

_____
_____
_____

★ Draw the best thing about today ★

List something that you

heard: _____

smelled: _____

ate: _____

☂ What did you see or do?_____

_____
_____
_____
_____
_____
_____
_____
_____
_____

Today's Overall Rating
☆ ☆ ☆ ☆ ☆

Note